P9-CQH-105

365 Things to Do with Your Kids

Before They're Too Old to Enjoy Them

BILL ADLER JR.

CONTEMPORARY BOOKS

Library of Congress Cataloging-in-Publication Data

Adler, Bill, 1956–
      365 things to do with your kids before they're too
old to enjoy them / Bill Adler Jr.
          p.   cm.
       ISBN 0-8092-2611-1
       1. Parenting.   I. Title.   II. Title: Three hundred
sixty-five things to do with your kids before they're too old
to enjoy them.
HQ755.8.A335   1999
649'.1—dc21   99-31190
                                                          CIP

Cover design by Kim Bartko
Cover and interior illustrations copyright © Laura DeSantis/
      Artville, LLC
Interior design by Susan H. Hartman

Published by Contemporary Books
A division of NTC/Contemporary Publishing Group, Inc.
4255 West Touhy Avenue, Lincolnwood (Chicago), Illinois
60712-1975 U.S.A.
Copyright © 2000 by Bill Adler Jr.
All rights reserved. No part of this book may be reproduced,
stored in a retrieval system, or transmitted in any form or by
any means, electronic, mechanical, photocopying, recording,
or otherwise, without the prior written permission of
NTC/Contemporary Publishing Group, Inc.
Printed in the United States of America
International Standard Book Number: 0-8092-2611-1
99 00 01 02 03 04 LB 13 12 11 10 9 8 7 6 5 4 3 2 1

To Karen and Claire,
who let me relive my childhood
with so much fun

Acknowledgments

I would like to thank those parents who contributed to this book—and their children, too: Peggy Robin (Karen and Claire's mom, and a published author herself), Bonnie Steinbock, Katharine McKenna, Amy Teschner, Michael Weiss, Martha Amitay, Deborah Buckner, Crystal Taylor, Shannon Lowder, Eleanor Dippel, Stephanie Carlson, Jennifer Merkel, David Gerrold, Pami Jo Evans, Ian Strock, Deborah Bova, Kelly Dunday, Sheila Blythe-Saucier, Tereson Dupuy, Jan Mason, and Kara Leverte, who contributed to this book not just as a parent but also as its editor.

Introduction

Time is precious. It's probably the most valuable and elusive part of parenting. One moment you have an infant, the next a toddler. Then one day, without warning, they say "mommy" or "daddy" for the first time. Blink and your child has gone from taking his or her first steps to riding a bicycle. The wondrous days of childhood pass so quickly.

This book is about enjoying your children's early years. It's about all those things that make childhood so wonderful for both kids and their parents. It shows you what you can do with your children to help make being a child magical and fun.

Since many of these activities are
transitory, reading about them may
make you feel melancholy; like a
rainbow after a storm, they only last so
long, and then they're gone. But 365
Things to Do with Your Kids is also about
making the most of your children's
tender years. In compiling this book I
talked with parents who told me about
what they most love to do with their
kids—and which activities they missed
the most once their children were too
old to enjoy them.

What makes happy, well-rounded
adults? The answer is a happy,
memorable childhood. This book is
about creating those memories.

But the activities in 365 *Things to
Do with Your Kids* aren't just good for

your children, and for your relationship with your children; they're simply great for grownups, too! Playing with your children—and playing *as* a child—lets you rediscover the wonders of childhood. It brings you closer to your children through shared experiences. It lets you grow with your children and remember what makes childhood so fun. The secret to youth isn't herbal medicine. It isn't exercise. It isn't even "thinking young." The key to a longer, happier, healthier, more fulfilled life is simply to see and enjoy the world with a child.

In the Rod Serling story "Kick the Can," several elderly residents of a senior citizens' boarding house decide to play a children's game called Kick the

Can, something they enjoyed as kids. They start running around, kicking a can, yelling, hooting, and otherwise acting childish. There was one holdout, however: a curmudgeonly old man who stubbornly refuses to engage in these childish antics.

The others go on playing without inhibition. They have fun, while the curmudgeon stays in his room, trying not to listen to the running around. Then the noises change from wispy, out-of-breath shouts to high-pitched squeals. His friends have changed— they've been transformed into children, with their whole childhood to enjoy again.

Reading this book might make you feel something like the people in that story. In *365 Things to Do with Your Kids* you will find a lot of activities that seem childish—but that's the point. This book is about re-experiencing your childhood through your children. It's easy to play games with your kids, to read them stories, to answer their questions about how autumn leaves change color. But it is an entirely different thing to peer behind your children's eyes and experience the same enthusiasm, wonder, curiosity, and unconditional love for their parents that make up a child's life. *365 Things to Do with Your Kids* will show you how to look at the world and experience life as if you were a child all over again.

Do you remember the first time you built a snowman? Or rode on a carousel horse? Or being tucked in tight while your mommy or daddy read you a book? Or climbed up the playground slide? There's nothing in an adult's life that can compare with how wonderful these experiences are to children. As parents, we all get to participate in these activities with our children. But wouldn't it be wonderful if we could do them all over again, as if we were children ourselves—to experience the pleasure of seeing a giraffe for the first time, sharing toys with your best friend, running around completely carefree, eating ice cream guilt-free, calling out for "mommy" and being protected, comforted, and loved?

There's a lot we can teach our children, but there may be just as much that our children can teach us. Childhood is a world of innocence, adventure, playfulness, creativity, wonder, and love—a world that we, too, can share in. It's one thing to help your children down a playground slide, or even go down the slide with your child on your lap. It's completely different (and vastly more fun) to feel the same exhilaration, the same "whee!" that your children feel as they coast to the bottom. It is one thing to answer (or try to) "Mommy, why is the sky blue?" But it is very different to re-experience hearing the explanation.

Children love—and need—to play. Play is an integral part of childhood: It *is* childhood. But as much as children like to play and have fun, they also like to do these things with their parents. While children are good at inventing games and activities, they *want* their parents to be the creative impetus behind many of these activities.

365 Things to Do with Your Kids is a collection of activities that your children will love to share with you— and that you will enjoy, too. It isn't about developing the child within you. It is about becoming a partner in childhood with your own children. It will make your children happier, too, because they will see the child in you. The activities included here will create memories that your children will treasure forever.

It is every adult's dream to relive the playful, carefree days of childhood.

365 Things to Do with Your Kids will show you how. You can share their childhood, have a more enriched family life, and feel like a kid all over again. So what are you waiting for?

1.

Pretend to be a horse and give them
rides around the house.

2.

Go hiking in the nearest forest or woods.

✓

3.

✓ **Teach them how to ride a bicycle.**

4.

Take them camping.   ✓

5.

Take them to a protest demonstration.

6.

Look at shooting stars.

The best times are around April 21 during the Lyrids meteor shower, around August 12, when the Perseids shower is in full bloom, around November 16 during the Leonids meteor shower, and around December 13 during the Geminids. Check your local newspaper or planetarium for the exact days and how best to view them.

7.

Take them to see the
area where you spent
your childhood.

8.

Take them to a pretzel
or cookie factory.

9.

Share your dreams, and interpret last
night's dreams together.

10.

Take them to see
the Fourth of July fireworks.

*Canada Day
Fireworks
& several
others*

11.

Volunteer for a class field trip.

12.

**Wake the children up before daylight
and take them to the railway station
the day the circus arrives in town.**
Watch their eyes widen with wonder as
the animals and performers disembark
from the circus train.

13.

**Read to them from *your* favorite
children's book.**

14.

**Build a snow fort and
have a snowball fight.**
Challenge your neighbors and
their kids to a snowball fight.

15.

Look at Saturn's rings and Jupiter's moons together.

On many autumn nights you can see Saturn's rings and Jupiter's moons with a medium-powered telescope. If you don't have a telescope (you should—they're not expensive and provide hours and hours of educational fun) then you can look for a local astronomy club, or visit an observatory, or go to a show at a planetarium. Besides Jupiter and Saturn (two of the sky's most fascinating objects), there's Mars, the Moon (the craters look spectacular with a telescope), nebulas, and galaxies to view.

16.

Watch *The Wizard of Oz* together.

17.

See a rainbow together (or just watch the rain).

18.

Go to the circus.

19.

Show them your office.

20.

Play Red Light, Green Light with your kids and their friends.

Here's how: Everybody stands in a line (except you) about 20 to 40 feet away. You turn your back and say loudly, "Red light, green light, one, two, three!" as quickly or slowly as you want. As you talk, the kids can advance. Once you stop talking and turn around they have to freeze like statues. Any kid you see who's still moving has to go back to the starting line. The first person to tag you wins.

21.

**Go through your family album or
boxes of old photos together.**

Don't just explain who's in the picture
and when and where it was taken. Let
your children ask the questions and set
the pace, pausing over people and
places that intrigue them, skipping over
parts that don't excite their interest.

22.

**Tell them a story about
something wonderful
that happened in your childhood.**

23.

Go to Disneyland or Disney World.

Take along a Family Radio Service radio, which you can buy at most electronics stores. These are small walkie-talkies that have a range of up to two miles. An FRS radio makes Disney World much easier (one parent can wait in line while the other grabs some shade, for example).

Visit a working farm.

25.

Take them to a parade.

26.

Make Christmas-tree
decorations together.

27.

Learn some magic tricks
you can amaze them with.

28.

Take them with you when you vote.

29.

Go to a baseball game.

30.

Talk about God.

31.

Wake them up one New Year's eve just before midnight (or let them stay up) to watch the new year come in.

32.

Save a large carton from a computer monitor or TV. Draw a door and then cut it out on three sides so that it will open and close. Draw a doorknob on the door. Cut out squares for windows and draw some shutters at the sides of the windows. Your children can decorate this playhouse and play in it until they're too big to fit in it anymore. Don't forget to play with them!

33.

Start a collection of something that both you and your child find fascinating. Some ideas: rocks, seashells, postcards, model trains, a glass menagerie, and, of course, stamps or coins. Remember, a collection doesn't have to be something you can keep in a box. It can also be something you write down: jokes, sayings, bumper stickers you've seen, and so on. When they pursue this hobby as adults, they will always think of you.

34.

Play imaginary stock market.

At the beginning of the month your family has a million imaginary dollars to invest in the market. Each person in the family gets an equal share of the money and can pick one stock to "buy"—as many shares as can be bought with his or her portion of the million. If you'd like, create a graph for each stock, so that you can see from day to day whose stock is up and whose is down. At the end of the month, figure out each person's imaginary profit or loss. Now figure out as a whole whether the family lost or earned money. Are you glad or sorry it's just pretend?

35.

Let them cook and serve you breakfast in bed on Father's Day and Mother's Day.

36.

Write a song together. Use a familiar tune and come up with your own personal words. For example, you could take the tune from "The Farmer in the Dell" and substitute your family name and hometown for the words: The Turners from Racine / The Turners from Racine / Hi ho the derry-o / The Turners from Racine.

Let them join you for your workouts and exercise. Not only will you both enjoy this, but you will be helping to instill a lifelong habit that your children will thank you for years later.

Valencia & Valerie

38.

**Have a serve-it-yourself ice cream
parlor and make yummy sundaes.**
Put out several containers of different
flavors of ice cream, along with little
bowls of toppings: rainbow sprinkles,
M&M's, chocolate dots, tiny jelly
beans—whatever the kids like best.
Slice some bananas and strawberries.
Warm jars of chocolate and caramel
syrup. Put out a can of spray whipped
cream. Put out scoops. Give them
aprons and let them go to town. Be sure
to join them in the eating.

39.

Snuggle up in bed or in a big, cushiony armchair and read them stories.

40.

Go someplace fun, like an amusement park or carnival, where you can get everyone's picture taken behind cut-outs of muscle-men and movie stars.

41.

Fly a kite. You can even make your own kites to fly!

Play "let's pretend" games with them.
Be a raccoon, a fairy, an angel, a
monster, an insect, a doll-come-to-life—
or whatever role you're cast in.

43.

**Make up a fantasy story
to tell them—with them in it.**

44.

Take home the classroom guinea pig
(or hamster, bunny, gerbil, etc.)
for the weekend.

45.

Let your children go out
and celebrate your wedding
anniversary with you at least once.

46.

Get up early and watch the sun rise.

47.

have watched Dolphis & seels etc feeding

Take them to an aquarium to see the shark feeding.

48.

Make the longest-ever colored-paper chain and hang it somewhere special.

49.

At Wild Water Kingdom Lazy River

Float down a river in an inner tube.

50.

Weny Weedie Weegie
Are u lonesome Tonight
Strangers in the Night Etc.

Share your favorite songs from the past with your kids: Frank Sinatra, Nat King Cole, Elvis Presley, old Beatles tunes, whatever you like best.

Make them a tape. You may find that these songs will become more popular with them than they are with you! You will be surprised how easy it is to get kids to become music fans if they know they are hearing *your* favorite songs. If you and your spouse have a song that you consider "your song," be sure to tell your kids that, and include it on the tape you make.

Truly by Lionel Richie & our Wedding Song was "Unchained Melody"

51.

Bake cut-out sugar cookies. Be lavish
with the colors and generous with the
sprinkles.

52.

*haven't tried
all but been
on quite a
few.*

**Spend a day trying all the swings in all
the playgrounds in your town.**

53.

**Put on some 1940's swing music and
dance around the living room like Fred
Astaire and Ginger Rogers.**

54.

Finger paint.

55.
Run through a sprinkler with them.

56.
**Make chalk pictures
on a sunny sidewalk.**

57.
Teach them pig latin.

58.
**Make popsicles and eat them
outside on a hot day.**

59.

Write a story about your family, each of you contributing a few paragraphs or a few pages.

Younger children can dictate, if they have not yet learned to write. The children should do the illustrations. To make a book cover (with adult help), decorate thin pieces of cloth-covered cardboard cut to just a little bit larger than the size of the pages. A printing shop will be able to attach the covers with glue-binding or spiral binding for a modest cost, or you may use a hole-puncher to make holes and then tie the book together with colorful ribbons or twine.

Val & VGG have done it but I hope to do it too.

60.

Make a birdfeeder. You can buy a kit
that is simple enough for small children
to put together. Or you can make one
yourself using an old soda bottle and
other odds and ends you find around the
house. Fill the feeder with seed, nuts, or
red-colored syrup (to attract humming-
birds), and hang it from a tree branch.
Or you might prefer to get the clear,
acrylic type of feeder that sticks to a
window with suction cups. Wait and
watch to see what types of birds come
to call.

61.
Play charades.

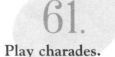

62.
Play Twister with your kids.
Last person not to fall wins!

63.
Play hopscotch.
Remember to lose.

64.
**Make a silly meal of foods
that are all one favorite color.**
Invite friends over to eat it.

**Decorate a shoebox together and
make it the family treasure box
for stashing mementos.**

66.

**Create a continuing story
with your kids.** The parent begins,
"Once upon a time there was a huge
dog named Bow-de-Wow who liked to
chase butterflies . . ." (or whatever
strange story line pops into the parent's
head). Then turn the story over to one
kid, who takes the story a little further,
and so on. This is a great car-trip
activity.

Plant a vegetable garden together.

If you don't have a yard,

plant a window-box garden.

Val & VGG have done it
but I hope to do it too

68.

Set up a family recycling center.

Have the kids decorate a cardboard box to create an attractive bin for storing newspapers to be recycled. Let them help you pick out containers that can be used for collecting bottles, cans, and other recyclables, and have them design labels for the containers. The kids should of course come along with you when you drop off the recyclables at the recycling plant (or perhaps just help you carry the recyclables to the curbside for pick-up).

69.

Give them a massage.

(Someday they'll give one to you.)

70.

On a frosty winter's day build a blazing fire in your fireplace, make hot chocolate with marshmallows, and play a board game or cards. If you don't have a fireplace, then draw one on a large piece of cardboard and put it against your living room wall. Pretending can be even more fun than having the real thing!

71.

Make a kitchen-sink pizza:
Buy a pizza shell and then let the
kids add anything they want: cereal,
hot dogs, peanuts, carrots, apples—
with or without tomato sauce.
Believe it or not, it always tastes good
and the kids love it.

72.

Sit on the floor opposite each other,
put your feet together, hold hands,
and rock back and forth, singing
"Row, row, row your boat."

73.

Be the first to teach them Cat's Cradle.

This is a popular game among kids in which a string is looped in a pattern like a cradle on the fingers of one person's hands and transferred to the hands of another so as to form a different figure. If you don't remember this game, chances are they can teach it to you!

74.

Kids & Val have done it

Find a really long hill and sled down it together.

75.

Lie in a hammock, look up at the trees, and listen to the birds.

76.

Pick violets— but not from someone's yard!

Kids taught me!

77.

Build a snowman.

Jump into piles of autumn leaves.

79.

Blow bubbles.

If your kids are young and new to bubble-blowing, just an ordinary, drugstore bubble mix and wand will do. If they're old hands at this, then move up to the next stage. Get a bottle of super-bubble mix (or mix your own) and a hoop-sized wand and blow giant-sized bubbles. You can also get wands that will form complex bubbles (multi-celled bubbles, or bubbles inside bubbles). For a really different and fun time with bubbles, go for a drive in a car and let the car's air conditioner blow the bubbles into the back seat where the kids are sitting—but keep those windows open!

80.

Carve Halloween pumpkins together.
Let your kids draw the design on the
pumpkin; you do the carving.

81.

Wash the seeds you take
out of the pumpkin, dry them,
roast them in the oven, salt
and spice them, and eat them.

82.

Watch the clouds and describe
together the animals, places, and
things that the clouds' shapes make.

83.

Sing their names in "The Name Game" song.

For this activity, you pick a name and sing it according to a particular tune and pattern. For example, if your child is William, you sing, "William William bo billiam, banana fana fo filliam, fee fie mo milliam, William!"

84.

Capture a caterpillar. Put it in a jar with holes punched in the lid, add some sticks and leaves, and watch it turn from a chrysalis to a butterfly or moth.

85.

Take them on a Ferris wheel.

86.

Build a house of cards. If you're having trouble getting beyond three or four cards, it's okay to notch the cards at the corners to make the structure sturdier.

87.

Divide your house or apartment into various "lands."

Your room may be called "Momanddaddia." The kitchen might be called "Fridgo-stoveland." If your child is named Tommy, his room might be called "Tommyland." Your daughter named Lauren might want to call her room "Laurenia." Each "land" has its own king, queen, or dictator, who makes the rules and exacts "tolls" for crossing over his or her land, and who can even decree what language is spoken there. Make sure that everyone understands before you start that this game is just for fun, that it has a definite ending time, and that when that time comes, everything goes back to being the way it was before, with the parents in full authority over all "lands"—and peace and open borders for all parties!

88.

Let them ride on
your shoulders.

Val has done it

89.

Let them ride on
your shoulders in the
swimming pool or ocean.

90.

Spot them as they
climb their first tree.

91.

Dye Easter eggs.

92.

done silently

Make wishes on a star, out loud.

93.

**Make a patchwork quilt out of bits
and pieces of clothing, blankets, and
other fabrics that have meaning to
different members of your family.**
Use your children's old baby blankets,
squares cut from your favorite flannel
shirt, your spouse's most beat-up pair of
blue jeans, maybe a bit of one of the
cloth napkins used at your wedding—
whatever you can think of that you
want to preserve in this special way.
The child who has trouble giving up an
especially loved but outgrown item of
clothing should be thrilled at the idea of
being able to keep it forever in the form

of a quilt. You can also have family photos transferred to cloth (just take them to any full-service printer/ photocopying place) or create your own fabric art using special permanent fabric markers, paints, glues, glitters, and other fabric decorations. The sewing of the quilt requires only the most elementary of stitching skills—it's something that can be done by any child old enough to use a needle safely. Once the quilt is done, hang it from a dowel on your wall and you've got a unique—and priceless—heirloom.

94.

Collect beautifully colored leaves in the fall. Iron them between sheets of waxed paper and frame them, or put them in a leaf-collection book.

95.

Give them butterfly kisses (eyelash brushing).

96.

Give them Eskimo kisses (nose rubbing).

97.

Make snow angels.

98.

Be the entertainment at your child's birthday party.

Be a magician, a gypsy fortune teller, a clown, or the <u>judge</u> of funny contests and silly games (three-legged races, wheelbarrow races, etc.).

Statue
Dance

Best
dancer
etc.

99.

Just do nothing with your kids.

in Wonderland & Centre Island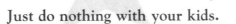

100.

**Take a rowboat or paddleboat
ride in a park lake.**

they taught me chess!

101.

**Teach your kids to
play checkers.**

*Chopstick Cuisine
Nandos — my favourite!
Silver Spoon — take out*

102.

**Have a favorite
family restaurant.**
Go there often.

103.

Hold their hands whenever you can.
You'll miss that later on.

104.

The next time your child asks you to come and see something right away, don't say you're busy, even if you are. Stop what you're doing and go see whatever it is your child is brimming over with enthusiasm about.

105.

Build things with blocks (which toddlers then knock down), then build them back up again together (and they still knock them down). Then they'll want to build them by themselves (and not knock them down!).

106.

When they're still too young to write, have them dictate a story to you.
If you can't type or write fast enough to keep up with what they say, turn on a tape recorder and later on put their words down on paper. Don't try to edit out their grammatical mistakes or change any baby words into real words—and definitely don't try to alter or even make sense of the plot. The charm of the story is in its pure childishness. Save the story and read it back to your child years later for a doubly enjoyable experience.

+ bubble tea!

107.

Make fruit smoothies.

Try out different fruits and fruit
combinations, such as blueberry,
strawberry, and banana.
Drink them in a fancy glass;
add sugar as needed.
Decorate with some special or
whimsical touch, like a little paper
parasol, or a maraschino cherry on a
tiny plastic toothpick sword,
or a swizzle stick with a monkey
climbing up it. (Just be sure
your kids are old enough
to know not to poke themselves
or each other with those
sharp-ended toothpicks!)

at Sheldon's wedding ✓

108.

Have your family portrait taken.

109.

Coach their team. ✓

110.

✓ **Participate as a family in a charity walk-a-thon.** Kids who are too young to walk a few miles can ride in a stroller or on your back in a baby carrier.

kids have done the Prostrate Cancer walk & I've done Mother Daughter walk with Valencia Wakman

111.

Take them to see Santa Claus. ✓

at Woodbine Beach once for a bit

112.

Take them to a jazz festival.
How many children do you know
who can sing be-bop?

✓

113.

Build a sand castle together.

114.

Take them to see a clown.

115.

Make neighborhood maps. Take a walk
with your kids around the neighborhood. Your children should write down
(or remember) the places they see.
When you get home create a
neighborhood map.

Humberwood

116.

**Go to a conservatory or arboretum
and enjoy the multitude and
variety of plants.**

Kia

117.

**Let them go with you to
a new-car showroom**
(even if you're only
window-shopping).

118.

Have a picnic by a lake.

119.

Organize a band of household instruments.

Make drums out of the rubber from disposable gloves stretched over empty, round oatmeal containers. Make banjoes out of old tissue boxes and gift-wrapping tubes, with rubber bands for strings. Make cymbals out of pan lids. Now parade around your house playing the instruments.

120.

Show them an old school
photograph and let them
try to spot which one of
the classmates is you.

121.

Ask them what *they* think
about something important—
something about how the
country should be run, or
what they think leaders
should do to try to eliminate
world hunger, and so on.

**Occasionally, just out of the blue,
say "I love you."**
Actually, do this more than
just occasionally.

**Talk to them about the love
you feel for your spouse,
or for your own parents.**

Knock knock

**Buy a book of kids' jokes
and teach them some new ones.**

125.

Find a newspaper from the day they were born and read it together.

You can look up old newspapers in the library, or go to visit the archives of the newspaper itself.

126.

Let them tell you jokes—and be sure
to laugh appreciatively no matter how
old and corny their jokes are.

127.

Cast their handprints in
wet cement, if you can,
or in plaster.

128.

Keep a door marked with their heights
and the dates they were measured.
Never have that door painted.

**Watch a sunset together on a hillside
overlooking the ocean.**

130.

When they're afraid, tell them about something that used to scare you when you were little but doesn't anymore.

131.

Kiss their boo-boos to make them better.

132.

Draw faces on the undersides of their big toes.

133.

Teach them how to snap their fingers.

134.

Teach them how to whistle.

135.

Watch them perform in whatever production they're in—school plays, pageants, recitals, talent shows—and be sure to stand up and applaud very loudly at the curtain call.

136.

Allow them to help you in the kitchen while cooking or cleaning. They can help with the easy jobs, such as pouring sugar into a bowl, stirring, watching the pot, and letting you know when the water is ready. Kids can help shape and knead meatloaf or pizza dough— just make sure they wash their hands before cooking, and *after*, too.

Sit around thinking up "what ifs:"
What if people had wings? What if you
had three wishes? What if our pets
could talk to us? What if we could go
anywhere we wanted tomorrow?

138.

**Look for four-leaf clovers
in a meadow.**

139.

**Read their fortunes from fortune
cookies—and then make up better
fortunes than the real ones.**

140.

**Set aside a large drawer or storage
space for your kids' artwork and
school papers.** Together, take a look at
what's in there now and then.

141.

Wash the car together on a hot day.
It's okay to get very wet and soapy.

not superlong

142.

**Find a playground that has a super-
long slide and go down the slide with
your child on your lap.**

143.

**Play Cave or some other game under a
blanket, with a flashlight as your only
illumination.**

happened last night!
Oct 13, 2012
with Valerie

144.

Let your son or daughter sleep in your bed with you when they have a nightmare.

You can let them stay the night, or carry them back to their own bed after they've fallen asleep.

145.

Let your kids teach you the names of all their stuffed animals— and teach you how each animal is related to the others (brother and sister, mommy and daddy, etc.).

146.

Host a sleepover. Read a story to your child and his or her friend.

147.

Make water balloons and toss them back and forth.

148.

Introduce them to Shakespeare, before they learn from school that it's supposed to be hard. You can read selections from Shakespeare's plays to them or you can retell the story of one of the plays in a way that suits your child's age. On Halloween you might recite the witches' rhyme from *Macbeth* (the part beginning "Double, double, toil and trouble / Fire burn and cauldron bubble")—especially if you're dressed up as a witch.

149.

Let them lick cake batter from the bowl before you wash it.

Though it may seem like a simple thing, watch those eyes light up when your child is presented with a big bowl with cake batter smeared along the sides! (However, don't do this if you have used raw eggs in the batter, because of the risk of salmonella).

150.

Get a pet together. Instead of extracting an undeliverable promise ("I promise to clean the birdcage or change the water in the fish tank"), make the pet a *family* pet, whom everyone has a hand in taking care of.

151.

Take them to a petting zoo or farm to see, touch, and feed the animals.

152.

Take them to the Ice Capades.

153.

Take them to a cemetery where you have family buried and tell them all you know about the history of their ancestors. Let them do grave stone rubbings, too.

154.

Pray with them at home. Teach them special prayers that have meaning for you.

155.

Let them make Rice Krispies treats. When the treats are finished, remember to save some for your children!

156.

Take them fishing. You do the hook and the worms. The kids do the fishing. If you don't intend to keep and cook the fish, then buy barbless hooks. Then it's a snap to free the fish, and it's fun to watch the escapee swim away.

157.

Camp out in the back yard in a pup tent with them. This is great fun for kids who are too young for a real camping trip.

158.

One day (but not the day you have that important staff meeting!) let them comb out your hair, pick out your outfit, or help you put your makeup on.

159.

Take your children to an old-fashioned county fair.

160.

Go canoeing or kayaking.

161.

Take a flight on a small airplane.
Call a local airport and find out if
there are any flight schools; there you'll
find a (safe!) instructor to fly with.

162.

Let them tell *you* a bedtime story.

163.

**Let them bury you in
the sand at the beach.**
Be sure to find someone
who can take pictures.

164.

Pull them in a wagon.

165.

**Write a letter to the President
of the United States together.**

166.

Think up a secret password that everyone in the family knows—and only the family knows.

This way, you'll be able to recognize the *real* family members in case somebody tries to impersonate one of you!

167.

Collect seashells at the beach.
Polish and display them.

168.

Walk along a riverbank or creek, looking for frogs and other animals.

169.

Paint portraits of each other (your children do one of you, and you do one of them). Repeat this every few years, and compare how the pictures change. You might want to turn a wall in your house into a gallery.

170.

Visit a nearby city and explore it by subway or bus.

171.

Go to an alpine slide that is open in the summertime. A really fun one is the Bromley Slide in Bromley, Vermont. Three different concrete chutes trace winding paths down Bromley Mountain—kids from age three and up love it. You take the chairlift to the top, then spend fifteen minutes sliding down wheeled sleds along the slide you have chosen for your age level and desired speed. Call 802-824-5522 or visit www.bromley.com for more information.

172.

Rent old television shows that you loved from your childhood, such as *The Ed Sullivan Show*, *The Honeymooners*, or the original *Star Trek* series.

173.

Volunteer to do trail cleaning or work at a soup kitchen.

174.

Go to the bank together, and explain how a bank account works.

Centreville
Woodbine Casino

175.

Take your children
horseback riding.

176.

Go on a hayride
together.

177.

Make mud pies.

178.

Make paper snowflakes and
hang them in your windows.

179.

Take your kids to the largest library you can find. Explore the stacks on different floors, pausing over whatever books catch your eye, learning things about whatever subject you happen to come across. Don't restrict yourself to the children's section. This outing will show your children that there's always something new to learn, and no matter how old you are, you can still feel awe at how much there is to know—and how much we still don't know—about our world.

North York Central Library

180.

Take a walk around your neighborhood looking for interesting objects: feathers, stones, leaves, twigs, dropped buttons, little bits of this or that. Paint the inside of a cardboard box lid green for forest land, orange or tan for desert, and blue for water, then arrange your twigs, stones, and other found objects in a way that suggests boulders, trees, boats, and other parts of the landscape or seascape of your imaginary country.

181.

Give your children a favorite old T-shirt to wear as pajamas.

182.

Plant a tree.

183.

Go though your house looking for toys and clothing to give away to needy children. Look for things you know that other children would really love to receive—not just old and broken stuff. Take the children with you when you drop off the toys at the receiving center.

184.

Attach two tin cans with a string and talk on this "telephone." How else are your children going to learn this fun way to communicate? (Make sure the string is taut or it won't work.)

185.

Play Faces.

The game goes like this:

"Show me your sad face."

"Show me your happy face."

"Show me your scared face."

"Show me your I-like-ice-cream face."

"Show me your pickles-and-sauerkraut face."

"Show me your I-want-a-puppy face."

And so on.

186.

**Take the dog to the park and throw
the ball or Frisbee around.**
If you don't have a dog, ask
a friend or neighbor if you could
borrow their dog. Any dog will be
happy to run after a Frisbee.

187.

Pick up food at a deli or fast food restaurant and have a spur-of-the-moment picnic.

188.

Go to a lake, river, or inlet to feed the ducks.

189.

Walk along a stream to find out where it starts.

190.

Visit a local news television show and watch it being aired.

(Call ahead for an appointment.)

191.

Play Monopoly.

192.

Go bike riding. If they're too young to ride a two-wheeler, take them in a bike trailer, or attach a child seat to the back of your own bike.

with Dad

193.

After you read a fairy tale, ask your children what they think about the characters and events of the story. Ask them questions about what might come after the story's ending. What if Sleeping Beauty decided she didn't like the prince who woke her up? Would they still get married? What about the wolf in *Little Red Riding Hood*? Was it really his fault that he was hungry and wanted to eat people? Let your child ask you questions about the characters' actions, too.

194.

**Buy—and send—
greeting cards together.** Better still,
get a computer program that creates
greeting cards and make cards together.
Even better than that—help your
children draw cards from scratch.

195.

Visit your state capitol or town hall.
Don't just tour the building; watch
legislative or city council debates
in progress. (If you can, travel to
Washington, D.C. to watch
Congress in session.)

196.

Go to a cat or dog show.

197.

Create and keep a family scrapbook. Both grown-ups and children should contribute to it. Put in the stubs of theatre tickets for performances you enjoyed, newspaper clippings about relatives or about things or places of interest to your family, postcards sent home from vacations, birthday cards that your kids have made or received, and all sorts of other souvenirs— as long as they can be glued or taped onto the pages of a book.

198.

Pan for gold or search for lost treasure. If there's no treasure spot nearby, bury some coins or toy jewels in your backyard.

199.

Go square dancing.

200.

Go to a Scottish clan gathering and watch the Highland games. There are Scottish festivals across the country; just check the weekly activities column of your local newspaper.

201.

cherries

Go to a pick-your-own orchard or berry farm and pick apples, strawberries, raspberries, or other fruits at the peak of their season. When you get the fruit home, start making pies, preserves, and other fruit dishes, and be sure to give lots of fruit away to your friends and neighbors.

202.

Make homemade ice cream on a hot summer day.

203.

Set them loose with a camera.

This way, you can see the world through their eyes—and it's also a creative outlet for them. Use a digital camera if you have one, because there's no film or developing costs. Another approach is to buy them disposable cameras. That way you don't have to worry if they drop the camera or get peanut butter on the lens. The pictures they take can become part of your kids' scrapbook.

204.

Dress up in old finery and have a tea party. Invite your child's favorite stuffed animals and dolls.

205.

Have your child's picture taken while posed on a pony.

206.

Make a rag doll and doll clothes from scraps of old fabric and yarn.

Build a tree house.

208.

Make a doll quilt or other doll-size accessories.

209.

On a rainy, miserable day spread out a checkered tablecloth on the rug and serve a picnic lunch indoors.

210.

Jump rope with them.
Teach them all the jump-rope rhymes you learned as a child.

211.

Really do up your house for Halloween.

Hang cobwebs everywhere. Get those little noise-activated, battery-operated gizmos that howl or make eerie sounds when someone comes to your door. Get light-up spooky eyes to peer through your shutters or curtains. Make your whole house seem like a haunted house, so all the children in the neighborhood will love to come to trick-or-treat.

212.

Go bird-watching.
Buy a bird identification book
so that you can know some facts
about the birds you see.

213.

**Let your child set the menu for dinner
one night** (within certain reasonable
limits that you set, of course). All right,
so you may end up eating dessert as an
appetizer or having french fries as your
main course, but you'll have a fun
evening, and it will be an interesting
change of pace from your usual fare.

214.

Every year on their birthdays write your children a letter telling them how much you love them; read the letters together when they are older.

going to do it for Valentine as his bday is coming up on oct 26/12

215.

Teach them how to make origami animals. You'll have to learn first yourself, but it's easy once you get the hang of it!

216.

✓ **Play Go Fish with your kids.** Children as young as three can play.

Give the dog a bath together.
Lots of laughing here. If you don't have
a dog, find a friend who does and offer
to help with the bath.

218.

When you go on a family vacation, always be sure to take lots of pictures. At least once on every trip, ask someone outside your family to take a picture of all of you together.

219.

Celebrate a half-birthday.

This is especially worthwhile for parents of a child with a late December birthday. At least once let your child have the experience of a celebration that is completely separate from any other winter celebration.

220.

Create a special family holiday over some event that is significant just to you, your spouse, and children.
For example, you could celebrate the anniversary of moving into your new house or the day your child overcame his fear of swimming and passed the test to go in the deep end of the pool. Invent your own ritual for the celebration—something beyond cake and gifts.

221.

Hold a family reunion.

222.

Have a cookout and make hot dogs and s'mores

(a treat made when you roast a marshmallow over a fire, place it on top of a thin piece of chocolate, and sandwich both the chocolate and the marshmallow between two graham crackers). If you don't have an outdoor grill at home, you can reserve the use of an outdoor grill at many public parks and campgrounds.

223.

Make puzzles of old pictures of your family. Glue an enlarged photo (at least 8-by-10) onto a piece of thin cardboard, then cut out oddly shaped pieces with an art knife or utility knife.

224.

Carve animals out of soap bars for them.

225.

Visit a local bakery to watch bread being made.

226.

Make wave bottles using colored water and oil and other liquids. Wave bottles are bottles with multicolored currents in them—they look like rainbow ocean waves. Put liquids in a clear, empty soda or water bottle. Let your kids suggest liquids.

227.

Make hand prints in plaster on paper plates; then paint and hang from ribbons.

228.

Let your kids teach *you* something.
Math they've learned in school,
an amazing fact about animals
that you didn't know, songs—
whatever they want!

229.

Make a candle in a milk carton with ice, wax, melted paraffin, and food coloring. Alternate dipping a wick in a solution of melted wax, food coloring, and a solution of cool water. The wick will magically become a candle as the wax adheres to it. Have a candlelight family dinner.

230.

Mat and frame their grade school art work. Together, gift wrap the pictures and send them to friends and relatives as presents.

231.
**Create the biggest
Lego building
you can make.**

232.
Go for a Sunday drive in the country.
Stop off at a farmers' market and buy
the freshest fruits, cheeses, and breads
for a wonderful roadside lunch.

233.
**Go to a water park and
go down a water slide together.**
Enjoy getting wet.

234.

Have a family scavenger hunt.
This is a good activity for when you're together with your extended family and there are lots of cousins around of varying ages. Divide into two teams, but make sure each team has about the same number of adults, teenagers, and younger children. Have an older relative (a non-player) come up with plenty of offbeat items—but nothing impossible!—and make sure that the lists are well balanced so that both teams start out on an even footing.

Build model airplanes, boats, or cars.
It's especially fun for both parents and
children if those models are more than
for display—if they can actually run
(whether by wind-up power or battery-
powered remote control).

**Watch Saturday morning cartoons
together.** Look over the TV schedule
before you start to find vintage cartoons
of the sort you enjoyed as a child. Avoid
the overly violent or insulting type.

237.

Make sure that at some point you all go to see the Grand Canyon. If you can only make the trip once, then wait until your children are old enough to be good hikers. It's really worth it to be able to hike down to the bottom of the canyon, stay overnight (either camping out or in the lodge) and hike back up on another day. (Make reservations *far* in advance if you plan to stay overnight.)

238.

Pick wildflowers and make garlands for the children to wear in their hair.

239.

Make macaroni jewelry. Use uncooked hollow pasta, such as elbow, penne, or fusilli noodles. Dye or paint the noodles different colors. Apply glitter or decorative glue, if you wish, and then string the noodles together to make necklaces and bracelets.

240.

Plan something that they can do to help alleviate homelessness in your town—gather old hats and mittens, take donations, or use allowances to buy an item. Go to a shelter to donate these things.

241.

Make pancakes with shapes.

Pour the prepared pancake batter into metal cookie cutters laid out in a well-greased aluminum pan. Don't use plastic cookie cutters because they will melt; and don't use a Teflon pan because the metal cookie cutter will scratch the finish. Young kids love Mickey Mouse, Barney, and other cartoon figures.

242.

Do a "leaf pounding." Tape a green leaf onto a board and cover it with a piece of muslin (cotton fabric, like the fabric used for sheets) taped securely to the board. Pound it with a hammer or shoe heel—whatever you want to use. The pounding releases the chlorophyll, which turns muslin green and makes a beautiful print.

243.

Help them write an autobiography. Include their first memories, their first teachers, their first playground experiences, their first dreams, etc.

244.

Let the kids decorate themselves to look like different animals. Have them wear bathing suits and give them either tempera paints, face paints, watercolor-based markers, or other washable colors. (Do this outside, as it can be messy.) This is great because it's normally a forbidden thing to do, and they will get a kick out of applying the paint to themselves. After they are finished painting themselves, squirt them all down with the hose to wash them off.

Be spontaneous. Do something on the spur of the moment that you haven't done before, such as visiting an old house, taking the subway or bus to the end of the line just to see what's there, going on a long walk with no planned destination, or flipping through a guide book on local attractions and going to see whatever is listed on the page where you flip the book open.

246.

Collect various insects, like centipedes, millipedes, "roly-polies," and other tiny creatures and look them up in a field guide to find out what their scientific names are. Let the creatures go free when you're done.

247.

Use your video camera and make a movie—not about your family, but a comedy, an adventure story, a mystery, or some other tale. Write a script ahead of time, but don't get glued to it. It's funnier if the actors depart from the script and start making up their own lines.

248.

Visit a new kind of museum—
a doll museum, a submarine museum,
a car museum—whatever you can
find that piques your interest.

249.

Red + white

**Wear matching clothes—the entire
family. Have your picture taken!**

250.

**Sign up together for the summer
reading club at your local library.**

251.

**Visit a greenhouse, then create your
own mini-greenhouse at home.**
Take a milk crate and put a plant inside.
Cover the sides, top, and bottom of
the crate with clear plastic wrap,
but have a few slits in the side.

252.

Visit a re-created historical town, such as colonial Williamsburg, Virginia, or New Plymouth, Massachusetts.

253.

Paint with pudding
(you can lick your fingers afterward).

254.

Have a squirt-gun fight (best to do this outdoors, when you're all in your bathing suits).

255.

Tell ghost stories around a campfire.

Do this when they're old enough to enjoy being just a little bit scared—but not *too* scared. (If they might have nightmares, then tell stories about friendly ghosts and good witches.)

256.

Make a super-size bowl of popcorn to share as you watch a rented video that the whole family can enjoy. (Choose a forgotten classic, like Danny Kaye in *The Court Jester,* or something that you wouldn't mind seeing again, like the original *Star Wars* or *E.T.*)

257.

Two words: bumper cars.

258.

Teach the kids to knit.

259.

Do a 1000-piece jigsaw puzzle
together, or do a giant
3-D jigsaw puzzle.

260.

Go to a free,
outdoor concert.

261.

Go bowling.

262.

Do a really messy craft
such as papier-mâché,
tie-dyeing, or candle-dipping.

263.

Plan an international dinner. Create costumes, flags, and posters to go with the foods of your selected country.

264.

Set up your own family website on the World Wide Web. If you're a member of America Online, Prodigy, Compuserve, or almost any other major Internet server, call your service to find out how to create your own website. Each member of the family can have his or her own page on the website and also suggest links (points of direct access to other web pages on the Internet) of particular interest to that family member.

265.

Teach the kids some really "groovy" dances:

the frug, the shimmy, the monkey, the swim, the loco-motion, the bus stop, the hustle, and, of course, the twist. If you don't remember how to do some of the dances, make up some motions, give it a name, and now you've got your own special dance.

266.

Visit a nursing home.
Bring some of your delicious homemade
cookies from activity number 51.

267.

Take a walk through a nature preserve with an experienced guide who can really open your eyes to the hidden animal homes around you—someone who can teach both the adults and the children things about nature that you never knew before.

268.

Go on a long car drive letting your children sing "99 Bottles of Beer on the Wall" from beginning to end without once begging, "Stop, stop, you're driving me crazy!"
(But don't let them sing it in reverse from zero back up to ninety-nine.)

Visit a paint-your-own pottery studio.
Instead of having each child do a
separate mug or dish, pick a large platter
and work on it as a whole-family
project. You could divide the item into
several sections, and have each member
design and paint his or her own section,
or one family member could do the
overall design, another do all the
lettering, another paint all the red parts,
and another paint all the blue parts—
whatever fits in with the talents and
inclinations of the artists in your family.
Present the finished product to the
grandparents as a special anniversary
gift, or keep it and display it proudly in
your own china cabinet.

270.

On the dreariest day in winter,
read seed catalogs, plan your
summer vacation, research summer
camps, and know that
this season, too, shall pass.

271.

Learn (or re-learn) with your family
how to hula hoop.

272.

On a hot day in July or August, go to
an indoor ice rink and skate.

273.

**Paint an unfinished toy chest or
bookshelf.** If your children are old
enough, supervise them while they
paint it or varnish it. Or let them use
wash-off markers to outline a design on
the wood that you will paint with oil-
based paints. If they are toddlers or
younger, the design could simply be
their handprints in different bright
colors over the top and sides of the
piece of furniture (in that case, use
washable latex paint!). For those with
more than one child, consider
decorating a piece of furniture for each
child to pass on to their own children.
That way your children won't fight over
who gets to keep the special piece of
furniture.

274.

Take your child with you when you give blood (but only do this if you can give blood easily, without saying "Ouch!"). Donating blood while your children watch helps instill in them a spirit of generosity.

275.

Explore the Internet with your child. Visit the Disney website, a public television site, or Yahooligans. You can play games, collect pictures of fairies and animals, and more. If you plan to leave your kids alone on the Internet, then it's a good idea to have a filtering program installed.

276.

During the dead of winter find an indoor pool and go swimming.

Your community may have an aquatic center, or try calling area health clubs or YMCA/YWCAs to find out if you are allowed to try out the pool before deciding if you want to join. Also, some hotels, universities, and YMCA/YWCAs with indoor pools allow fee-per-swim use of their pools.

277.

Enter a product contest together. It could be a drawing, like one of the big magazine distributors' contests or a create-a-recipe contest (send in your idea for a new dessert made with a certain brand of whipped topping).

278.

Put on a show together. It could be something you just come up with on the spur of the moment, like playing "air guitar" and singing, or it could be a big production that you plan together and spend weeks to produce, with home-made scenery, costumes, and a real script.

279.

Go through the newspaper to find an inspiring story your child can understand. You may need to check the paper regularly for a few days until you find a good one—such as an article about an animal rescued by the fire department, or children who come up with some novel way to raise money for a good cause.

280.

Late one evening go outside for a game of flashlight tag. Playing flashlight tag is easy—you tag the victim by shining the beam of the flashlight on them.

281.

Unplug your TV
for a weekend and do
whatever you want!

282.

Talk with your kids about when you were "bad." A good time for this is when your child does something wrong. Instead of yelling at them, or sending them to their room, think about something awful that you did at the same age, and what your parents did to punish you. Tell your child about what happened to you. Talk about how you were punished by your parents. (Your children will find this fascinating.) Besides being an interesting activity, it's likely that your story will make a more lasting impression on your kids than a harsh punishment.

283.

Invent a new dish made of an unusual combination of different foods. Each member of the family gets to name one ingredient to go into the creation. Give the dish a long, fancy French name, like Medallions de Chien Chaud avec Fromage Americaine a la Maison des Feldman (Sliced Hot Dogs with American Cheese at the Feldman's House).

284.

Find a penny from the year of your child's birth. Shine it with copper cleaner till it sparkles and give it to them.

285.

Play Ha-Ha with your children.

This game will be more fun if you can recruit a few of their friends to join in because more is better—but you need a minimum of four players. Each player lies on the floor with his or her head on another player's tummy. The players form a circle so that the last person to lie down is next to the first person, who can lay his or her head on that player's tummy. The first player says, "Ha." The next player says, "Ha ha." The third player says "Ha ha ha," the fourth one says "ha" four times and so on around the circle.

The object of the game is to try *not* to laugh a real laugh but to make someone else laugh. When everyone has finally laughed for real, the game is over. Some games only last a few seconds, because no one can avoid craking up the first time they hear "ha" while lying on someone else's tummy.

286.

**Teach your children some
easy hand-shadows.**
A bunny can be made with two
fingers raised over a fist. For a
butterfly, hook your hands together at
the thumbs and wave your "wings."

287.

Rent an inflatable moon-bounce unit.
It's a good idea to get together with your
neighbors and rent it for your whole
block. Then the adults can finally get a
chance to bounce with their kids.

288.

**On the next family birthday, don't buy
a cake. Bake one from scratch!** Let the
birthday child choose the type of cake
and icing, and do much of the
preparation. Definitely let the child play
a big role in the cake's decoration.

289.

Next Halloween, go trick-or-treating as an ensemble.
Pick a theme and plan everyone's costume around it. For example, a big family could do the Wizard of Oz. A daughter can dress up as Dorothy, and other family members can be the Scarecrow, the Tin Man, a Flying Monkey, a Munchkin, or any of a number of other choices. A good choice for a baby or toddler is the Cowardly Lion, because a lion suit is so easy to make and so comfortable

for a little one to wear. Just get a
tan flannel sleeper-suit and sew
on a lion's tail. Use face paint to
do the lion's nose and whiskers.
Add a woolly cap with ears sewn
on, and a big mane of brown
yarn, and you have it. Mom can
be Glinda the Good Witch or
the Wicked Witch of the West,
and Dad can be the Wizard. Of
course if you have a dog (or any
four-legged pet) it should wear a
collar that says "Toto." Another
approach would be for everyone
to dress the same, for example,
all as Raggedy Ann's and Andy's,
or all as lumberjacks, or
members of a baseball team.

290.

Memorize a long poem together, something fun like "The Owl and the Pussycat" or "'Twas the Night Before Christmas." Or you might try to find a poem about something that has special meaning for your family (for example, if someone in your family is named Annabel, learn Edgar Allen Poe's "Annabel Lee," or if your family loves baseball, all of you learn "Casey at the Bat"). You might want to do the poem together at a family gathering or holiday celebration.

291.

Try walking on stilts, or pogo-stick jumping.

292.

Go to the beach in the winter.
Take off your boots and socks and
touch your toe to the water.

293.

Have a week-long contest called Stop Saying. . . .

Each member of the family picks a bad speech habit, something you wish you didn't say so often, and tries for a week to avoid it completely. It could be saying the word "like" (as in, "He's, like, a really nice guy") or attaching the question "Okay?" to the end of every sentence.

But it doesn't have to be any particular word; you could decide to avoid using all vulgar words, or the children could agree to avoid calling each other names or saying things to pick fights with each other. It could even be a certain tone, such as ending each phrase with a rising note so that it sounds like a question. Keep score of how often each person uses whatever it was they were supposed to stop saying, and at the end of the week, declare a winner. If all week long everybody is able to stick to the "Stop saying" rules, then you might want to continue the game indefinitely.

294.

Let your child keep her favorite stuffed animal, no matter how old or worn it becomes. Sew back any parts that rip and mend any holes that develop. Your child will be glad you did.

295.

Learn a few classic lullabies.
Sing your child to sleep with "Mama's Gonna Buy You a Mockingbird" or "All the Pretty Ponies."

Rockabye Baby

296.

Make lunch faces. On a round slice of baloney or salami, put two halved black olives for eyes, a diced piece of celery for the nose, and a small wedge of tomato as a smiling mouth. Carrot or cabbage shavings can be used to make hair; so can a ruffled piece of lettuce. You can also take individually sliced pieces of American cheese and cut out holes for eyes, nose, and mouth. The kids can put the faces between pieces of bread and eat them as a sandwich, or eat them as finger-food straight off the plate. You can also act as a ventriloquist and make the faces "talk" to the children (of course they'll say something like, "Oh nooo, don't eat me!" and then the kids will eat them right up).

297.

Play a memory game.

A good one is I'm going on a trip. The first player says, "I'm going on a trip and in my suitcase I'm packing an apron" (or any item beginning with the letter A). The next player has to remember that item, and then add one beginning with the letter B: "I'm going on a trip and in my suitcase I'm packing an apron and my binoculars." The

third player repeats everything
and adds an item beginning
with the letter C, and so on,
with each turn making the list
of things longer to remember. If
your children are young, keep
the items simple and easy to
repeat, and don't worry about
whether they'll fit in a suitcase.
Let them take along an
elephant for the letter E. If
they're older, tighten up the
rules. Say they have to come up
with an item that might really
be useful on a journey to a
particular place—and put a time
limit on each turn.

298.

Put funny, surprise notes in their
lunch boxes.

299.

When you and your spouse (or any other adult) are out walking with your child between you, each take one of the child's hands and on the count of three, lift the child up as you keep walking for a few steps.

300.

Teach them tongue-twisters—the harder the better. Try "Rubber baby buggy bumpers." Or "Black beetles' blood." And, of course, "She sells seashells by the seashore."

301.

Make your own family
"coat of arms."

Draw a shield shape and divide it into
sections, one for each member of the
family. If your family totals four, then
make an X across the shield, or a + to
divide it into quarters. For a family of
five, insert a center section. For a family
of three, divide it vertically, like the
French tricolor flag. Now think of a
symbol to go in each section to
represent each member of the family.
One might choose a favorite animal;
another might choose an object used in
a hobby (for example, a shovel for a
gardener or a racket for a tennis player).

Choose a color scheme for the shield, keeping in mind that simpler is usually better—you don't want it to look garish or cluttered. Perhaps use one color for the background and a contrasting color for the object in one section of the coat of arms, and then reverse the two colors in the next section. Finally, choose a motto to go at the bottom. Latin is traditional, but any language—or even your own made-up family code—can serve the purpose. Once you have a design that represents your family, you might even sew a family flag to display on holidays, or have your coat of arms printed on your stationery or made into emblems to be embroidered on a set of matching blazers that you can all wear.

302.
Ride an old-fashioned
carousel with your children.

303.
Go to see an air show
or a flying circus.

304.
Paint your children's fingernails all different colors.
Let them paint your fingernails
whatever colors they want, too.

305.

Get some Silly Putty.

Get the Sunday comics section of the newspaper. Show them how to flatten the Silly Putty and cover one of the panels of the comics and then find the picture printed on the Silly Putty as you lift it from the page. Then watch the picture stretch out and fade away as you pull the Silly Putty apart.

306.

Count the freckles on
your child's nose.

307.

**Catch fireflies and put them in
a jar with air holes in it.**
Talk about some of the things you
could do if you had a million fireflies.
You could light up your house.
You could make them spell out your
name in big letters. What else could
you do? Make sure you let the fireflies
go at the end of your evening.

308.

**Hang a prism in a sunny window and
make rainbows inside your house.**

309.

Tell them stories of the Greek myths.

You might want to skip over some parts (some of those gods and goddesses had very complicated love lives!) and emphasize the adventure (Theseus going into the labyrinth to fight the Minotaur, Icarus and Daedalus making wings to fly away from the palace where they were imprisoned, etc.). Be guided by your child's age and ability to understand.

310.

**Take them with you
when you visit a relative or friend
who's in the hospital.**

311.

**Go for a walk after dark and
listen for the sounds of crickets
chirping and owls hooting.**
Watch carefully during summer
to see if any bats fly overhead
(which is common in certain
parts of the country).

312.

Plan a really elaborate trick for April Fools' Day. For example, a few days before April Fools' Day, give your child a small stuffed animal—but make sure it's one that comes in a much larger size. A few days ahead of time, tell your child that it seems as if the animal has been getting a bit larger each day. The night before April Fools' Day, remove the animal after your child has gone to bed and replace it with the larger version of itself. This trick will really be a hit if your child sleeps with the stuffed animal in her bed, and wakes up the next morning to find the animal has really grown!

313.

Skip with your child.
Kids love to skip, and would love to
see you do it, too. They may not
believe you know how.

314.

Instead of buying gifts for their teachers, help your children make a gift. They can make bookmarks, pencil cups, picture frames (you can insert a class photo if you have one), potholders, or tote bags. You may want to use a craft kit or materials that you already have around the house, but however you do it, be assured that your teacher will appreciate the effort that went into the creation much more than receiving yet another store-bought candy dish in the shape of an apple.

315.

**Teach them
hand-clapping games.**

For babies, do Patty-cake, but change
the alphabet letter to the letter that
starts your child's first name, and
change the last line to insert your
child's name and complete the rhyme.
So instead of saying: "Pat it and roll it
and mark it with a C / And put it in the
oven for baby and me!" you would say
(for a child named Karen, for example):
"Pat it and roll it and mark it with a K /
And put it in the oven for Karen all
day!"

akar bakar bambay bo

316.

For older children, teach some elimination games.

The children put out their fists and you tap each fist, going around in a circle as you chant:

Engine engine number nine

Going down Chicago line

If the train should skip the track

Would you get your money back?

One, two, three, you are out!

The last fist you touch on the word "out" must be withdrawn. When only one fist is left, that child is "it."

317.

Show your child how to do mirror writing (writing backward so that when you hold the paper up to a mirror, the words are displayed correctly).

318.

Leave cookies and milk out for Santa.
Be sure to eat them yourself
before your kids get up
in the morning;
on Christmas it's pretty much a
certainty that your children
will be awake well before you are.

319.

medieval times with valerian & valencia

Go to a medieval or
renaissance fair.

320.

Rock together in a
rocking chair.

321.

Push your child on the swing
as high as you can, for as long
as the child wants to swing.
(That can be a very long time.)

322.

Tell your child about some other fairies besides the Tooth Fairy.

There are Tangle Fairies who visit at night and make tangles in your child's long hair. There are Star Fairies who collect the wishes that you make upon a star. There are Fireplace Fairies who live in the embers and make those crackling, hissing, and popping noises when they want to startle you. Sometimes they even try to throw out a hot ember to get your attention. You can also invent fairies that have interesting new powers. If they're afraid of getting shots at the doctor's office, for example, tell them about the shot fairy that will leave a treat under their pillow that night.

323.

If you have more than one child, be sure to set aside some time to do something special with each child individually—something that is geared to that child's particular interests. Do this even if your children are identical twins.

Fly around the house. Everyone sticks their arms out and "flies" around making airplane noises, landing, crashing, picking up passengers, and offering in-flight entertainment.

**Do the "Hokey Pokey"
with your kids.** Then do the "Limbo"
(how looo-ooow can you go?).

326.

Make a train.

Your family lines up, one behind the other, hands on the hips of the person in front of them. The lead person is the engine and the last person is the caboose. Snake around the room saying, "Chugga-chugga, chugga-chugga, whooo-whoooo!" Take turns being the engine, boxcars, and caboose.

327.

Give your old clothes to your kids for dress-up. Be sure to take their picture after they've got themselves all dressed up.

328.

Hold your child up by the ankles so that she can walk on her hands.

329.

Roll down a grassy hill together.

330.

Stand up with your legs apart and let your baby or toddler crawl "under the bridge." If they're walking, they can *run* under the bridge.

331.

Make homemade lemonade and set up a lemonade stand on the corner.

332.

Twirl around as many times as you want. Stop, and watch the room keep twirling.

333.

Take a plain paper grocery bag and cut out holes for eyes, nose, and mouth. Give your child some yarn to glue on to add hair or fur, and give them bright markers to decorate their mask as a robot, animal head, or whatever. A long gray sock stuffed with tissue paper makes a good elephant trunk. While your child makes a mask, be sure to make one for yourself.

334.

Write a fan letter together to someone
you and your child both admire.

335.

Have a secret handshake or "hi" sign that only members of your family know. Here's one: As you shake hands, using your middle finger, gently scratch the other person's palm. Here's another: During the handshake tap the back of the other person's hand three times with your thumb. Make up your own secret signal.

336.

Play music by blowing through a blade of grass held tightly between your thumbs.

337.

Form a jug band. One of you should play the kazoo, another blow into an old jug, somebody else play a pennywhistle, and at least one of you drum your hands on your knees or on a tabletop. Everyone sing a country or folk song. Cousins, grandparents, aunts, and uncles make good audiences.

338.

Watch your children while they're sleeping. While this isn't something that you really do *together*, seeing your children asleep so soundly is a memory that *you* will want to keep.

339.

Teach your child some useful mnemonics. To help them memorize the colors of the rainbow in order, for example, the name Roy G. Biv (every letter in that name is the first letter of every color—red, orange, yellow, green, blue, indigo, violet). To help them remember how many days are in each month, teach them the rhyme "Thirty days has September, April, June, and November / All the rest have thirty-one / Except February, which is fine / With twenty-eight days / (In leap years twenty-nine)." To help them with spelling, teach them: *I* before *E* / Except after *C* / Or when sounded like *A* / As in "neighbor" and "weigh."

340.

Create
a family
time-capsule.

You can buy a kit in a science
store, or you can make your
own from a rust-proof metal
container. Good things to put
in your time capsules are
photographs, newspaper articles,
lists of favorite things (books,
music, activities), tape cassettes
of your voices (just hope that in
the future the cassette player

doesn't become obsolete!) and whatever else your family would like to find in the future to remind you of the way things were in the past. Put a watertight label on the time capsule saying who put it there and when it is to be opened, and then bury it in your backyard. Be sure you leave instructions in a way that won't be forgotten, so that a decade from now (or a quarter-century, or half-century—whenever you've chosen to have your time capsule unburied) you'll know how and where to retrieve it.

341.

If your child is having trouble falling asleep, tell him how to have a good dream. What you do is describe a wonderful dream to your child while holding a hand to his forehead, so that the good dream will pass from you into his head. Then, as soon as he's asleep, he will have that dream, fresh and ready to be dreamed.

342.

Build a sand city at the beach or in a really large sandbox.

343.

**Hold your child's hand during the
scary part of a movie or play.**
If your child leans over to tell you it's
not necessary, say, "But *I'm* scared. I
need to hold *your* hand."

344.

Get into a swimming pool with them and show them how *they* can carry *you*!

345.

On a rainy day, have raindrop races. Each of you pick a drop at about the same height at the top of a window pane. The first person's drop to drip down to the bottom of the pane is the winner.

*Family art class
paint a tree with a
red robin*

346.

Take a class together. It could be an
arts-and-crafts class, a karate class, an
aerobics class—whatever you think your
child would most enjoy doing along
with you.

347.

**Get down on the floor with your
crawling or toddling child.**
Let your child direct
how you play together.

348.

Bake a loaf of bread together. Don't use a bread machine—make it from scratch. Read your child the directions, but let your child do the mixing of ingredients, the kneading of the dough, and as many other tasks as you think your child is ready to handle. Then everybody sit back and wait for the wonderful aroma of baking bread to fill the house.

349.

Measure your child's hand against your hand, and feet against your feet.

350.

**When your birthday
(or your spouse's birthday)
is coming up, make a suggestion
for your child to give an "action"
present, rather than something
wrapped up in a gift box.**
For example: a song that your child
would sing to you (and not just
"Happy Birthday to You"),
a poem or dance that your child
has made up for you, or a skit that
all your children might act out.
Let them use their imagination
to come up with something that
expresses how they feel.

351.

Have a Backwards Hour
in which one day, for one hour,
the child gets to act like the parent
and the parent like a child.

352.

Talk about what you would do if you
had one hundred million dollars.

353.

Talk about all the great things
you would still have if you didn't
have any money at all.

354.

Find out when and where the nearest American Indian pow wow is. Throughout the year there are American Indian festivals and dance shows that travel around the country. Even before they are old enough to understand the narration that explains the action, children can appreciate the color and grace of the tribal ceremonies and come away with an appreciation for America's first inhabitants.

Write a contract with your child over something important.

For example, in your contract your child might agree not to try smoking before age 20 (since virtually all smokers begin the habit in their teens), and you agree that on that birthday you will provide a much-desired reward. Let the reward for the contract fulfillment be something that is appealing to the child at the age of the contract signing, but also something the child might reasonably still want years later—for example, a trip to a Caribbean island. Have the child write the contract in his or her own handwriting, sign it, and date it in front of witnesses. Each child in the family may want to write his or her own contract, spelling out an important promise to be kept at least until a specified date, for his or her own designated reward.

356.

Bounce them on your knee.

357.

Call your local fire station and find out when they have an open house to show off the firehouse and the fire engines to children. If they don't have an annual open house, find out if firefighters visit schools or children's clubs to talk about fire safety and arrange for a visit.

358.

Explain an important event in the news to your children. Let them ask as many questions as they like until you are sure they understand the issue. Use your best judgment when picking the news story.

359.

When your child shows you a picture she's drawn or a Play-Doh sculpture she's made, don't just nod and say, "That's nice," or whatever you usually say. Take time to study it and comment on it the way an art teacher might do. Praise the specific things about the art work that you think are imaginative, or well executed, or full of feeling. Give your child the sense that you really are interested in her work and encourage her to keep expressing herself artistically.

Listen to classical music with your child. A good introduction to classical music for children who haven't heard it before is the video of Disney's *Fantasia*. (You can fast forward through "A Night on Bald Mountain" if you think that segment might be too scary for your young ones.) Your children also might like "The 1812 Overture" with its cannon-fire, or Beethoven's 9th Symphony with its "Ode to Joy" chorale.

361.

Play Musical Chairs. This game works best with a large number of children, so let your children invite their friends. Put out a line of chairs equal to the number of players. Now take away one chair. Start the music. Everyone skips around the line of chairs. Suddenly the music stops, and everyone must find a seat. The one left standing is "out" for that round. To keep that young child involved, appoint him or her the job of starting and stopping the music. A CD player with an easy-to-operate remote control works best. Take away one more chair every time another player is "out." Continue playing until only two players and one chair are left. The person who sits in it when the music stops is the winner.

visited the sikh temple

362.

Take your kids to the religious services of a friend who is of a different faith from your family. Let them learn about the diversity of ways in which people worship God.

✓

363.

Get into the habit of corresponding with your children whenever you are away from them. If you go out of town on a business trip, even for the day, write them a letter or a postcard. If they go off to stay at Grandma and Grandpa's for a weekend, let them know you'd like to get a letter from them, too.

364.

Answer their questions about the natural world. If you don't know why the sky is blue or what makes the tides ebb and flow, then borrow a few books on science from the library and read until you know enough to give solid answers to your kids' questions.

365.

Think up your *own* ideas for things you'd like to do together before your children are too old to enjoy them.